BLACK HOLES AND REVELATIONS

Black Holes And Revelations

 Alfred

Produced by
Alfred Music Publishing Co., Inc.
P.O. Box 10003
Van Nuys, CA 91410-0003
alfred.com

Printed in USA

ISBN-10: 0-7390-7990-5
ISBN-13: 978-0-7390-7990-4

Front Cover Design and Photography by THE MEN OF MYSTERY
Artwork by DANMANDELL
Band photos by Derrick Santini. Air Force Photo (no endorsement intended)

Arranged by Alex Davis
Edited by Lucy Holliday

musemanagement.co.uk
muse.mu

 Contents printed on recycled paper.

TAKE A BOW

Words and Music by Matthew Bellamy

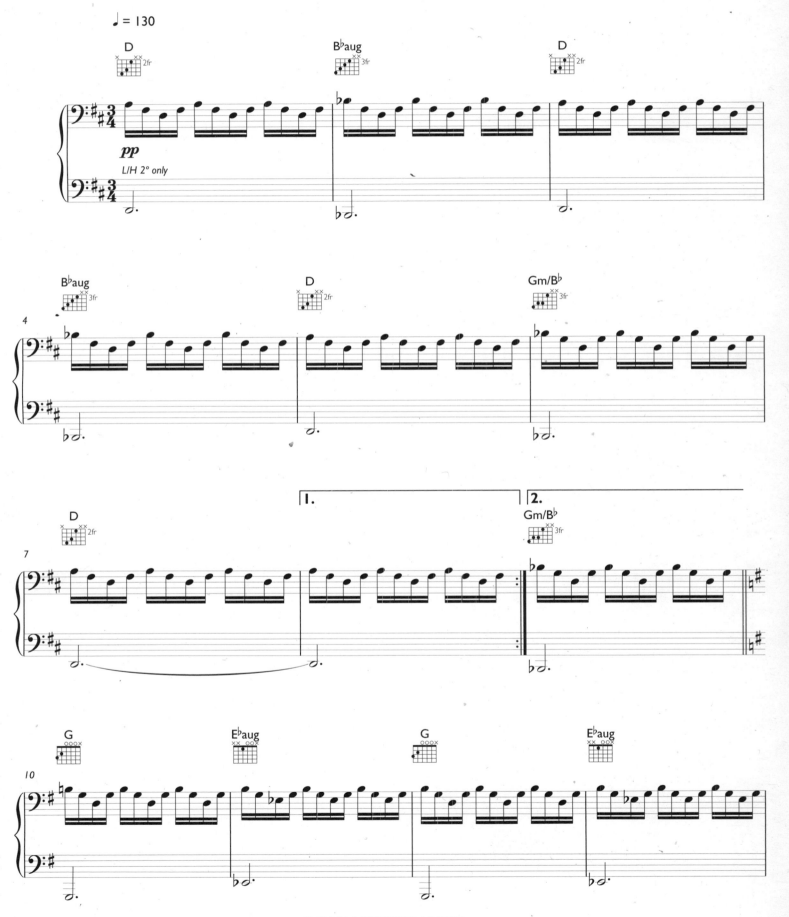

a   bow.

beg for___ their lives___ and___ their___ souls.___ And

burn, you will___ burn, you will___

burn_____ in hell,___ yeah___ you'll burn_____ in hell,_____ you'll

STARLIGHT

Words and Music by Matthew Bellamy

SUPERMASSIVE BLACK HOLE

Words and Music by Matthew Bellamy

1. Oo___ ba-by don't you know___ I suf-fer,___ oo___ ba-by can't you
2. I___ thought I was a fool___ for no-one,___ oo___ ba-by I'm a

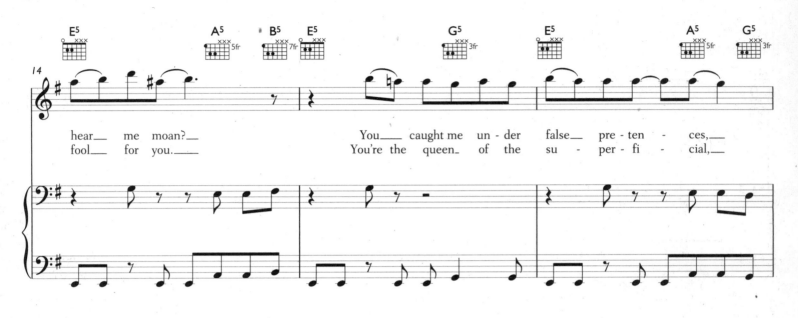

hear___ me moan?___
You___ caught me un-der false pre-ten-ces,___
fool___ for you.___
You're the queen___ of the su - per-fi - cial,___

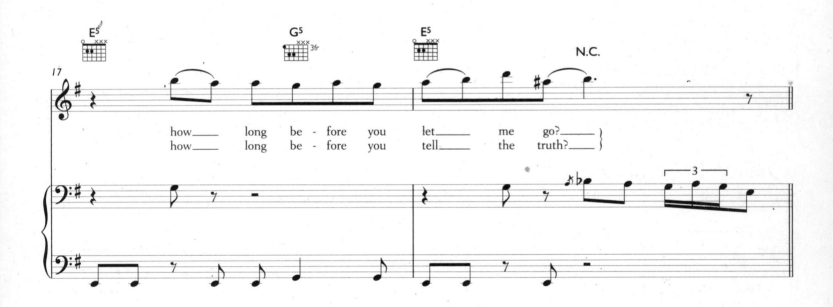

how___ long be - fore you let___ me go?___
how___ long be - fore you tell___ the truth?___

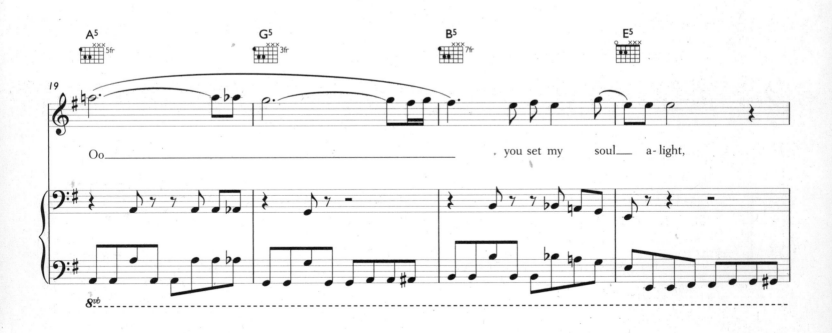

Oo_____ , you set my soul___ a-light,

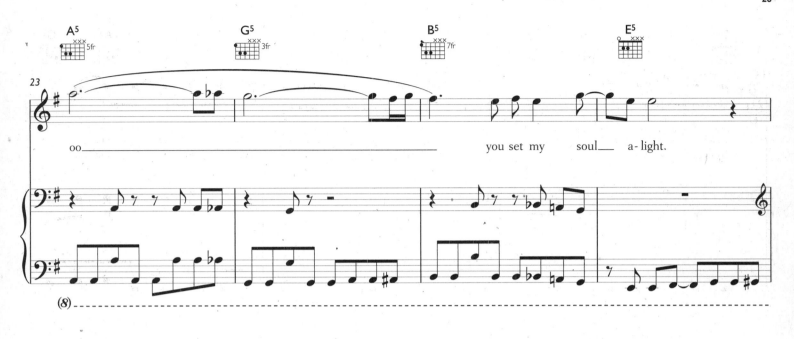

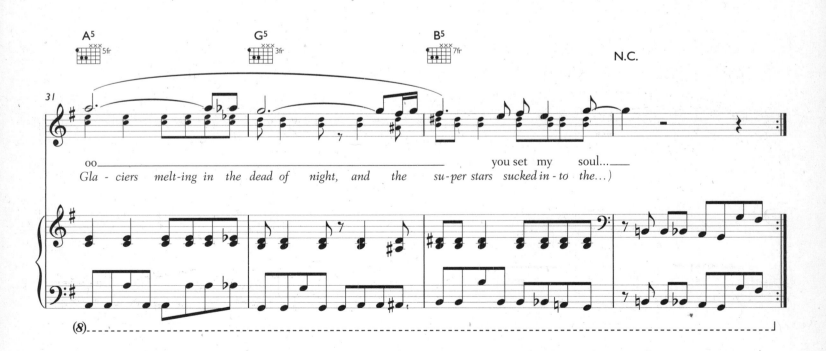

It's a su-per-mas-sive black hole,___ a su-per-mas-sive black hole,___

a su-per-mas-sive black hole,___ you're a su-per-mas-sive black hole.

Fine

N.C.

MAP OF THE PROBLEMATIQUE

Words and Music by Matthew Bellamy

1. Fear_____ and pan - ic in__ the air,_____ I want to
2. Life_____ will flash be - fore__ my eyes,_____ so scat - tered

be free_____ from de - so - la - tion and des - pair.__ And I
and lost_____ I want__ to touch the oth - er side.__ No -

Lone - li - ness be o - ver?____

When will this

SOLDIER'S POEM

Words and Music by Matthew Bellamy

INVINCIBLE

Words and Music by Matthew Bellamy

1. Fol - low_____ through, make your___ dreams come_____ true, don't give up
2. Do it on your own, it makes no___ dif - ference to me, what you___

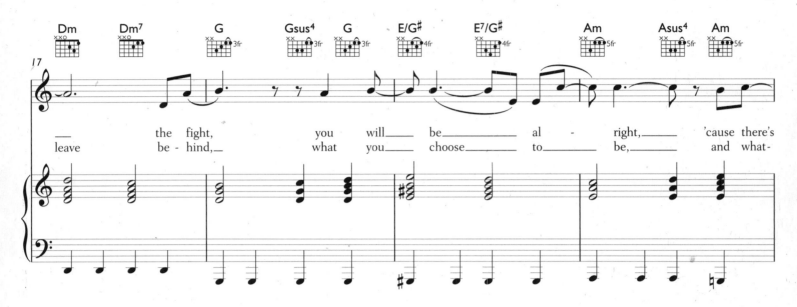

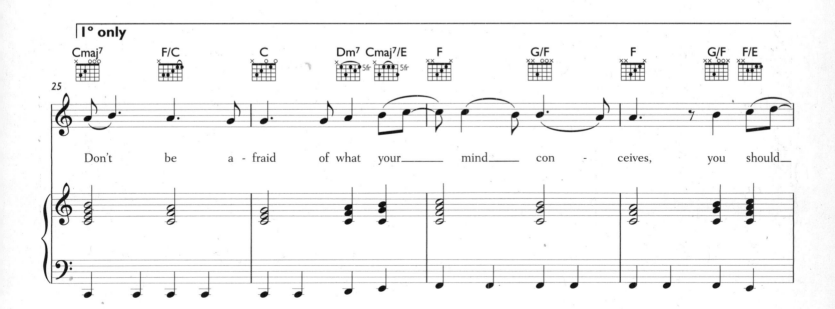

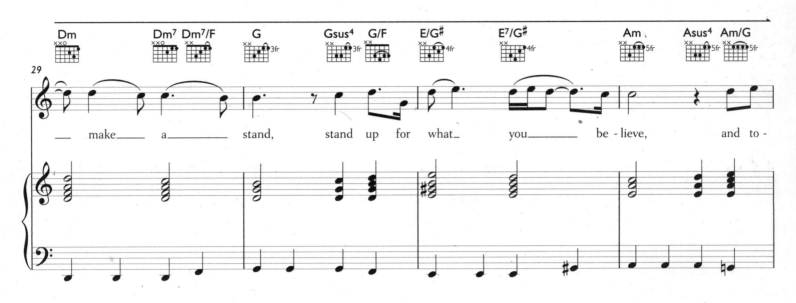

make___ a___ stand, stand up for what___ you___ be - lieve, and to-

-night___ we can tru - ly say to-ge-ther we're in - vin - ci - ble.___

Dur - ing___ the strug - gle they will___ pull___ us down,___

Small notes 2° only

mf

but please,_____ please let's use____ this chance to

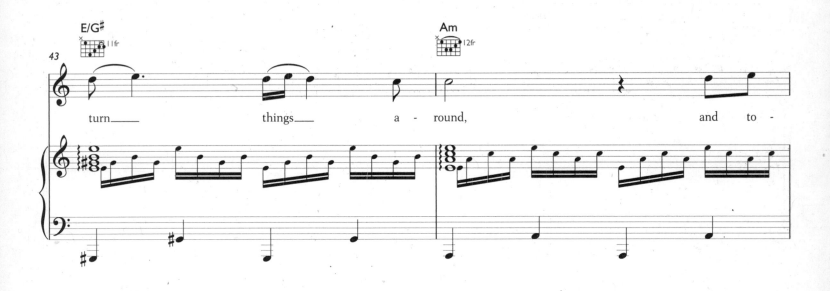

turn____ things____ a - round, and to -

-night_____ we can tru - ly____ say to - ge - ther we're in -

-vin - ci - ble,_____ to - ge - ther we're in - vin - ci - ble.____

Dur - - ing___ the___ strug - gle they will pull_____ us_____

down,_____ but please,___ please_ let's_ use___ this chance to___

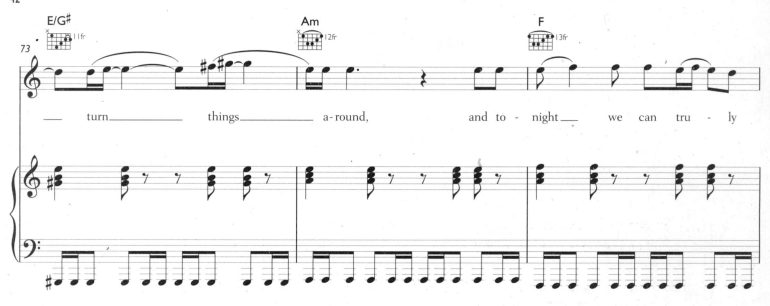

turn_____ things_____ a-round, and to - night___ we can tru - ly

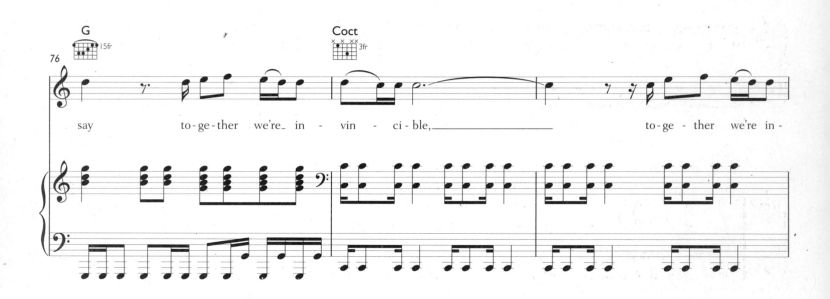

say to-ge-ther we're_ in - vin - ci - ble,_____ to-ge-ther we're in-

-vin - ci - ble.

ASSASSIN

Words and Music by Matthew Bellamy

EXO-POLITICS

Words and Music by Matthew Bellamy

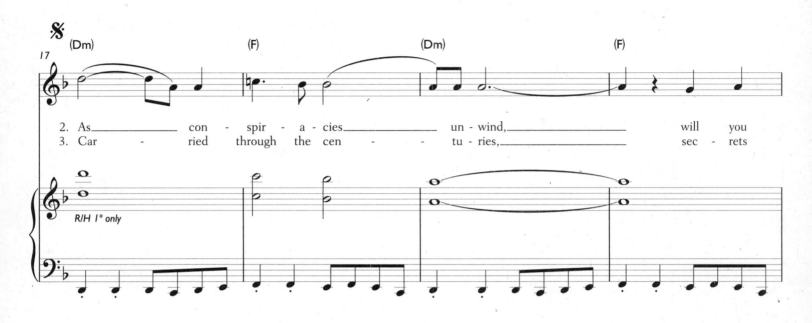

2. As _____ con - spir - a - cies _____ un - wind, _____ will you
3. Car - ried through the cen - - tu - ries, _____ sec - rets

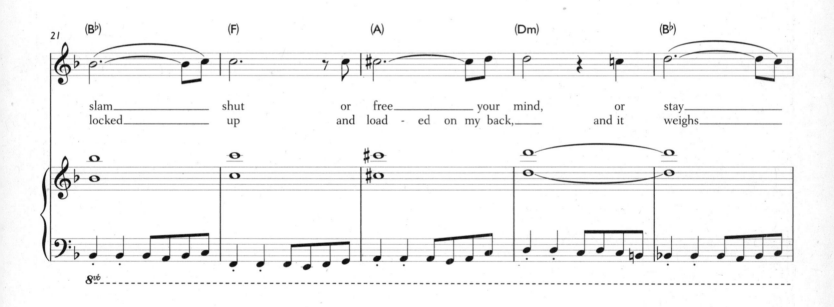

slam _____ shut or free _____ your mind, or stay _____
locked _____ up and load - ed on my back, ____ and it weighs _____

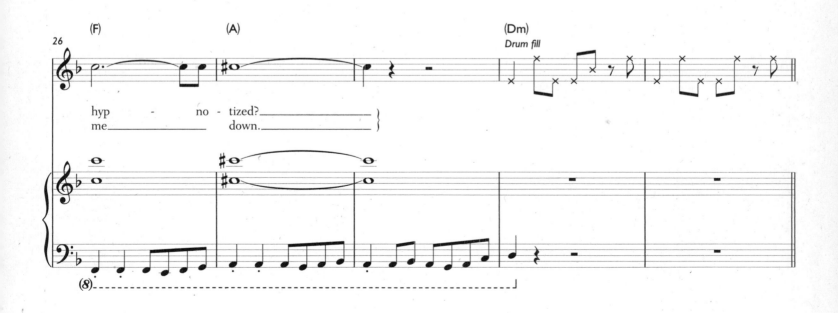

hyp - no - tized? _____ }
me _____ down. _____ }

CITY OF DELUSION

Words and Music by Matthew Bellamy

3. You will not

HOODOO

Words and Music by Matthew Bellamy

Come in-to my life,__ re - gress in-to a dream, we will hide

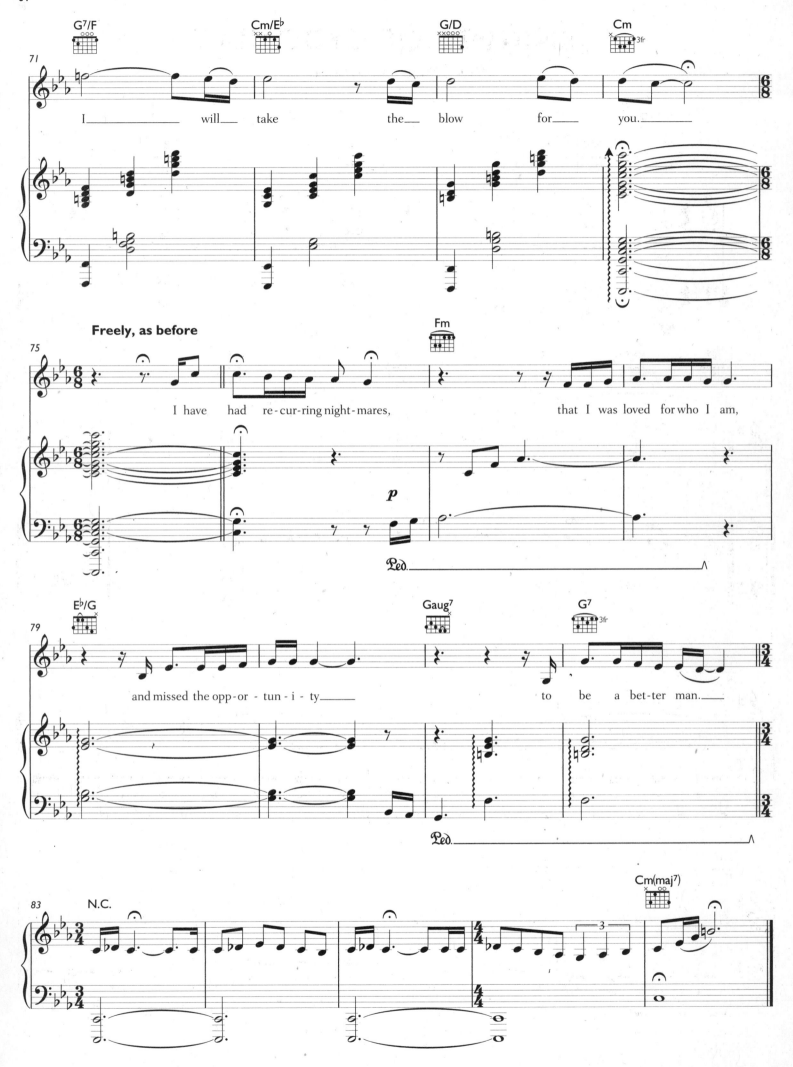

KNIGHTS OF CYDONIA

Words and Music by Matthew Bellamy

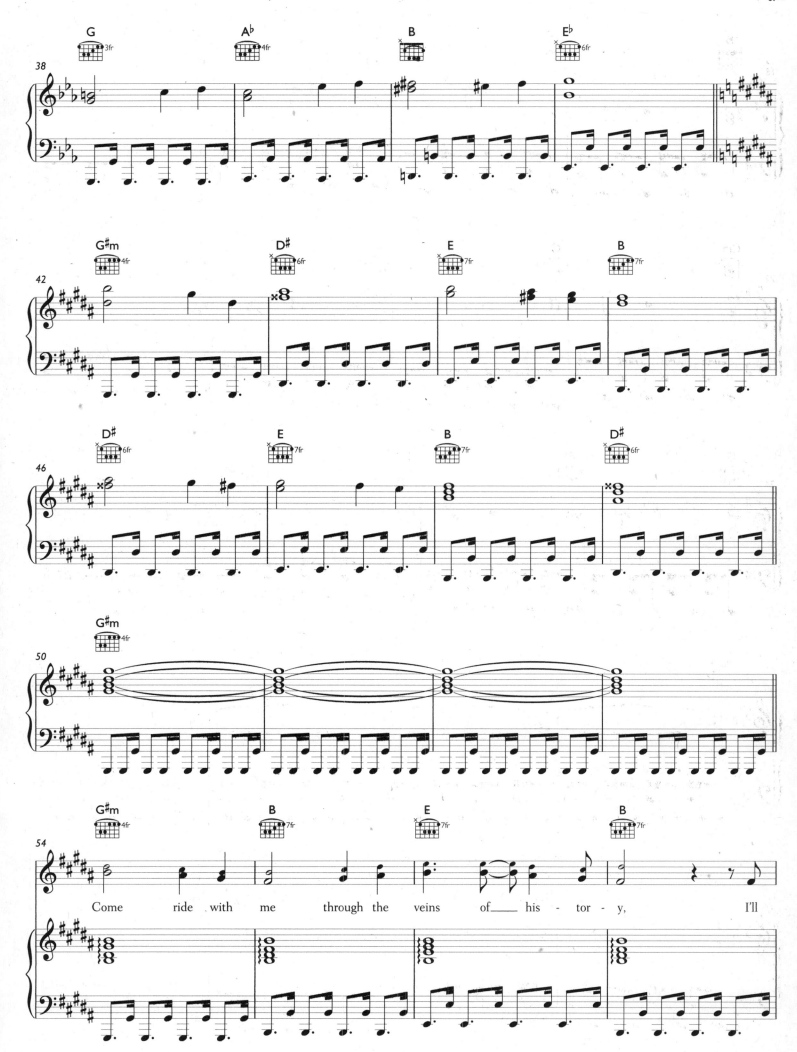

Come ride with me through the veins of__ his - tor - y, I'll

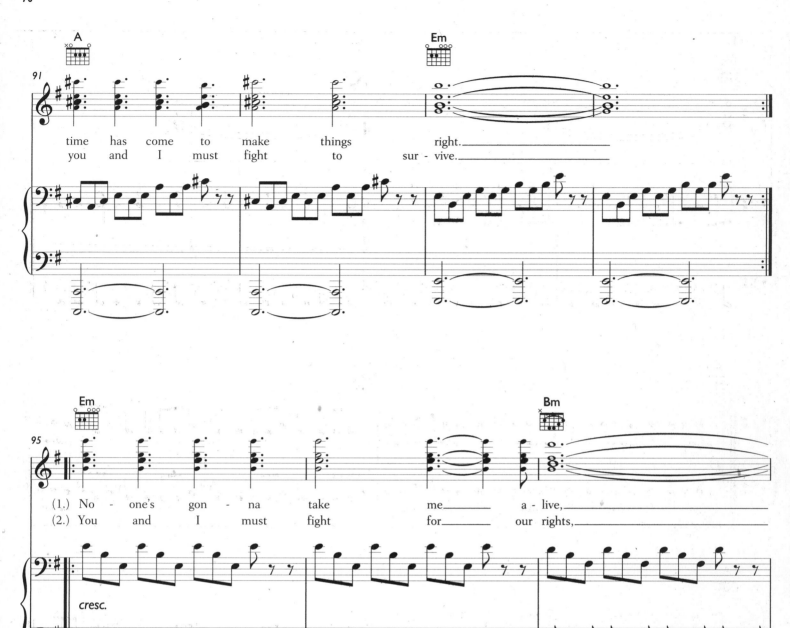

time has come to make things right._____
you and I must make fight to sur - vive._____

(1.) No - one's gon - na take me_____ a - live,_____
(2.) You and I must take fight for_____ our rights,_____

cresc.

_____ the time has come to make things
you and I must make fight to sur -

time has come to make things right._____
you and I must fight to sur - vive._____